Postcards From a Dream

Poems by Johanna Ely

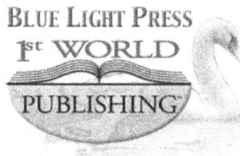

BLUE LIGHT PRESS
1st WORLD
PUBLISHING

San Francisco | Fairfield | Delhi

Postcards From a Dream

Johanna Ely

First Edition.

ISBN: 978-1-4218-3648-5

Library of Congress Cataloging-in-Publication Data

1ST WORLD LIBRARY
PO Box 2211
Fairfield, Iowa 52556
www.1stworldpublishing.com

BLUE LIGHT PRESS
www.bluelightpress.com
Email: bluelightpress@aol.com

Author Photo
Hedi Desuyo

Cover Art: Painting by Sam Morse, acrylic on canvas.

For Sam, whom I love beyond words,
and for my son, Russell,
who has shown me that with determination,
dreams do come true.

Acknowledgements

With gratitude to poet and Editor-in-Chief Diane Frank, who taught me how to fine tune my work and encouraged me to publish my first full length collection of poetry with Blue Light Press.

Many thanks to Sherry Sheehan for proofreading my final manuscript.

Grateful acknowledgement to the following journals and anthologies in which some of these poems were previously published: *Artists Embassy International, Autumn Sky Poetry Daily, California Quarterly, MockingHeart Review, The Ina Coolbrith Circle*, and *The Poeming Pigeon*.

I would also like to thank my dear friends in the Benicia poetry community who read and listened to my poems and offered their generous support and feedback.

About the Author

Johanna Ely is the author of two chapbooks, *Transformation* (2015) and *Tides of the Heart-Poems for Benicia* (2018). She is an award-winning poet and had a poem nominated for a Pushcart Prize in 2018. She has been published in many journals and anthologies, including *The Poeming Pigeon* and *California Quarterly*. Johanna served as the sixth poet laureate for Benicia, California. In 2018, she collected poems written by the Benicia First Tuesday Poets and put forth the anthology, *Light and Shadow*, published by Benicia Literary Arts. She hosts the monthly series, Poetry Inside Out, inviting poets from all over the Bay Area to come to Benicia and read their work. She also enjoys writing ekphrastic poetry and has coordinated many ekphrastic readings at the local galleries.

Contents

The Night We Saw a Meteor 3

Sway To... 5

Writing Poetry is Not Like Gardening 6

What Still Matters 7

The Letter 9

Spring 10

First Day of Spring in the City Cemetery 12

The Bud 14

Tulips (3 haiku) 15

Spring Evening 16

Song in the Key of Summer 17

Plums 18

August 20

Labor Day at Live Oak Park 21

Autumn Red 22

First Rain 23

Fog 25

Listening to the Trees 26

Flying In 28

Returning to Lodi to See the Sandhill Cranes 30

After Hearing That the Camp Fire is Almost Contained 33

Mountain Lion 35

Two Hawks 37

Ode to Basho 39

Inside Out Love 41

Your Hands 43

Birthday Poem 45

Afternoon Nap 47

Roots 48

After the Poetry Reading 50

Forecast 52

I Bring You Roses 54

Lovers in the Red Sky 56

After Seeing a Painting by Monet 58

A Geisha's Lament 59

The Muse 60

Dream Poem for Li-Young Lee 61

Postcards From a Dream 64

Books 65

Palm Reader 67

A Room of One's Own 69

Water Lilies 72

Isabelle 74

The Gift 76

It Wasn't Your Fault 78

How the Dream Comes 80

How to Celebrate my Life 83

Transmigration 86

Your Voice the Sound of Waves 88

In Memory of a Poet 90

Prayer 92

As This Day Fades 93

A Tiny Bird Called Hope 94

Postcards From a Dream

The Night We Saw a Meteor

It was late August,
the air warm enough
for us to sit outside,
to watch the soft darkness
cover the trees.
Still new with each other,
we felt a silence settle between us
and were amazed
to see a burning ball of light
streak across the sky —
a falling star gone
before the wish.
We wondered if it had crashed
in a field west of us,
or disintegrated
before touching the ground.

We shared a moment of awe
that stays with me even now.

Seven years later
we are not who we were then.
Our cells have been replaced,
and we have decayed
and regenerated many times
in our own small cosmos.
Yet, our bodies
still shimmer with meteor dust
billions of years old —
our bones made from exploding stars.

Sway To...

What begins in the heart—
the beat, beat, beat
of life pulsing through veins.
Every river that winds
toward an open sea.
Reeds that bend in water
ecstatically toward dappled light.
Scales that slither,
diamonds that shimmer,
circles and spirals that spin.
Sway in your silky cocoons—
Wrap yourselves
in the colors of
ochre fields,
mossy forests,
indigo mountains,
copper skies.
Sway to the music
you've always known.
Break open—
become a thousand butterflies.

Writing Poetry is Not Like Gardening

I don't want to plant tiny seeds
that fall out of shiny packets showing
pretty pictures of daisies, marigolds, pansies.
Each kernel carefully placed and watered,
inches apart from the next,
coaxed to grow and behave
the same as all the others.

I want to discover the prickly burr
that sticks to my sock,
the ochre pod caught in my hair,
the hundred dandelion seeds
clinging to my jacket like opened parachutes.
Give me something hard to pick off,
seeds that are unruly and tenacious.
Give me what survives in the dark woods
or scrambles along a sea cliff.
Let me pull from my body
what is untamed and unsettled
and fling bright, bold words across the page,
wildflowers for the taking.

What Still Matters

The water stain
on the dining room table
still remains —
a perfect circle left
from the vase of irises
I received on my fortieth birthday.
That, and the table,
lined and scratched
like an old man's face,
remind me
there is a beauty to aging.
All these millions of years,
water tumbling over riverbeds,
the ragged rocks thin and clean,
smoothed into glass stones,
scarab green,
or wind howling in the crevices
of ocean cliffs,
how it erodes and softens them,
dunes of bone white sand, rising.
All that once came
kicking and screaming
into this nascent world,

weakened to a whisper —
the veneer chipped,
worn to a thin gold band,
takes on its own polished patina,
while a voice low, far away,
murmurs what still matters —
how the purple tongued
irises turned
a deeper indigo
in the waning light.

The Letter

In January, the afternoon
folds neatly into itself—
blank and dull as a piece
of flat gray paper fitted
into a plain gray envelope—
wordless
sealed up
unsent.
Address unknown.

Who can read
the calligraphy of winter,
the fine strokes of emptiness,
or remember the black outline
of small birds now missing in icy branches?

How can I bear to leave
the envelope fixed firm,
the signs of a distant spring unwritten,
or not wonder why this day
(though sunless and unmarked)
has been left to disappear
unopened?

Spring

spring
has come
and flung
herself
upon this tired world,
extremely wet
and green behind the ears,
the daffodils aflame.
she came
last night
and sang herself a tune.
the little old balloon man
whispered her sweet name.
she came
and
tumbled
rumbled
into rain.
spring
has birthed herself
upon this weary world,
bright eyed and winter wise,
she collates leaves on trees.

the bees
mistake her for a rose.
the rain knows
spring has come
and
the world,
all lily lost
and dewy eyed,
will never be
the same.

First Day of Spring in the City Cemetery

It's spring in the city cemetery—
lupine blooming wild
with their cones of purple blossoms,
dandelions with spiky leaves
growing at the foot of toppled headstones,
poppies, cups of gold,
dotting the gentle slopes.
I sit on a wooden bench—
feel the warm sunlight on my face,
see the Carquinez Strait gleaming in the distance,
hear the trains rumble.
I am not here to visit a loved one—
I just want to feel peaceful.

The dead have no words.
I wonder if they know
the change of seasons—
or listen to the rain
tapping on the ground above them,
the trees singing prayers to them.
Do they hear me whisper
how much I wish I'd known them,
or sadly admit

that life goes on without them?
I have all afternoon to sit
among the wildflowers and the dead—
to wait, to listen,
to understand
what can't be said.

The Bud

That moment of anticipation,
when a single bud is beginning
to crack open—
only the tips of
pink petals emerging,
still streaked with the newness
of caterpillar green.
Wrapped in a scarlet cocoon,
a flame is unfolding—
still holding inside
thin, pink fingers
of petals that carefully
uncurl and separate,
reach up to caress light.
The primordial secret of life
that will soon be told again
by this unnamed flower,
a mystery ready to burst and bloom—
this first breath of spring
longing to exhale.

Tulips

1.

Six weeks until spring —
the pink tulips sag their heads
tired of waiting

2.

Rainy Kyoto —
geishas twirl pink umbrellas
at the next bus stop

3.

I shake the pink bells —
ring them so long and so clear
they wake up my heart

Spring Evening

A sigh of remembrance
as I drive home.
The fields on this side
of the freeway
still flower green,
as the moon, almost full,
rises over the soft, brushed outline
of cows dotting a hillside.
Clusters of oak trees
darken to a deeper hue,
as long, thin clouds drift
across a grey sky —
a last gasp of brilliant pink
fading in the west.
To the south,
Mt. Diablo's peak is hidden,
reminiscent of Mt. Fuji.
Another beautiful woman
hides her tears,
behind an evening cloud bank
of forgetting.

Song in the Key of Summer

How easy to praise
the beauty of this summer day,
to hum off key,
compose a symphony.

White hydrangeas
larger than whole notes
float above the fence,
the treble clef merely
a cloud placed in the middle
of a morning glory sky.

Noisy crows clang bravado.
Roses shudder and sigh
like small red violins.
In the wind,
blue agapanthus shake
their wild tambourine heads.

My heart when I see you
beats a hummingbird's thrum
and plays a tender scarlet melody,
a song I have sung,
no matter what the season.

Plums

I like them best just picked,
still warm from the sun.

Every year at the end of June,
the plums ripen all at once
and become the fruit of excess.
Neighbors deliver them to me
in stained, brown lunch bags,
not questioning need or want,
but politely demanding their fruit be taken.

This season, the plums arrived
just before a summer party.
I rinsed them carefully in cool water,
patting each one dry.
Then felt their perfect roundness
in my hand, as I placed them gently
in the blue ceramic bowl,
a still life for Cezanne.

They looked too beautiful
to be eaten —
these purple jewels of summer.
By evening,
I too, was giving them away,
asking guests to take some home —
five or six to a plastic bag,
until one plum was left.

There are certain things
I can never get enough of —
a billion stars in the sky,
a hundred red roses blooming at once,
my lover's kisses, warm and wet.
But this one plum was all I needed,
sweet juice on lips and tongue,
a harvest of desire.
The taste of all the days of summer
in my throat.

August

Here is the end of summer:
the green heron's solitary stance
as he preens on a rock
uncovered at low tide.
How the geese circle and honk
in grey light, over grey water.
Your fingers stained red
from blackberry bushes —
the same color as autumn leaves.
Every August, the geese with their
melancholy call,
and the blackberries, so sweet.

Labor Day at Live Oak Park

The huge stone fireplace
almost touches the redwood trees —
patches of grey sky moving through boughs.
We admire the laying of the rock,
the tall, solid chimney built by hands
that have disappeared.
Here, in this quiet Berkeley park,
where a trickle of creek runs alongside
the six picnic tables,
our tribe gathers again to share food
and words we have labored to write.
I wonder what it was like
so many years ago —
the fire blazing all night long,
sparks and words exploding —
those brilliant falling stars.

Autumn Red

In trees all over town,
dozens of scarlet handkerchiefs
wave farewell.
That blazing autumn red —
how it flutters,
then drifts down
into beaks of migrating birds,
nests of busy squirrels.
A color even brighter
than the hummingbird's flaming head —
or the shade of lipstick that I wore
that fine October day
when we last met —
the color of regret.

First Rain

When the first rain comes,
let there be a distilled charm
in its voice,
a sad song sung dolce
about smoky fires
and fading October light,
the tempo adagio.
Let it sigh and bow
to the steady applause
of the wind.

When the first rain comes,
let there be no rankling
from the fallen leaves
which squirm and swim
like shiny red carp
caught in grey puddles.
Let their mouths sing
silent cantos in Chinese.

When the first rain comes,
let the soggy bougainvillea
wail in purple tongues,
answer questions never asked.
Once, we were distracted
by the wet scent of longing.
Now, whatever song we
wanted so badly to remember
will pour down —
the name of it
just drops of water
tapping,
tapping,
against the pane.

Fog

It's not a cat after all,
but a seductive siren
who suddenly appears—
her smoky eyes as cool and distant
as the winter hills hidden in the curves
of her grey satin gown.
She sings jazz at the bar,
caresses the piano keys,
croons torch songs to the sailors
in her low throaty voice,
and leaves a silky white ribbon
on the Old Coast Road
for a lover to follow.
He winds his jag slowly
along the dark ocean cliffs,
trusting her until the ribbon disappears,
and the brake light ahead
glows as red as the tip of a cigarette
held between her fingers—
wisps of her dancing in his headlights,
beckoning him to follow.

Listening to the Trees

I listen to the trees —
their language garbled
through roots that snake underground,
ancient telephone lines running
from one sentient being to the next.

I listen to the Japanese maple
shyly open its new leaves to sunlight,
and the eucalyptus with its shaggy bark
leaning forward into the bright white
of tumbled clouds.

I listen to the tall pine
stretch its stiff limbs,
aching after the cold winter
as the flowering plum sighs
and flaunts its soft pink petals.

I listen to the trees
sing lullabies to the birds,
welcoming every squawking chick
to this jubilant season —
robins picking twigs from their branches,
the trees cradling nests in their arms.

I listen to the trees
walk silently,
their dark green bodies
moving across golden ridges
as the afternoon light travels west.

Flying In

There's a strange frenzy in my head
Of birds flying
Rumi– The Book of Love

Near sunset
our bus crept down
the narrow road
and we parked next to
some flooded fields
glistening in the last breath
of a cold silver November light,
the outline of marsh grasses
still sharp and defined,
the sky still blue
with wisps of smoky grey.
We settled on the benches
behind the wooden blind,
squawking and flapping
like old mallards ready
to roost for the night,
and waited impatiently
for the cranes to fly in.
At first, a trilling sound,

the rolling sound of r on the tongue,
a calling of one to the other.
Then they came in pairs,
in groups, in flocks,
hundreds of dark winged beauties,
silhouettes against the softening dusk,
flying straight as arrows
towards the safety of water,
the promise of warmth
and camaraderie under a sickle moon.
We remained silent for a long time,
even after the sky became empty and quiet,
knowing that a great love had just
swooped down into the fields
of our lonely hearts,
a living song, a noisy affirmation,
the cries of a thousand cranes
rising into one love, one voice.

Returning to Lodi to See the Sandhill Cranes

Three years later
I return to the wetlands
to witness the Sandhill Cranes
fly in at dusk —
to hear their comforting trills,
to remember their language,
how they once spoke to me.
I watch the smoldering sun
burn a round scar
in the cigarette ash sky,
as it slowly drops into the smoky horizon.
I am here to seek out the cranes,
the way a woman dying of thirst
searches for drops of water
at the bottom of a cup —
my face, the pallor of bone dust.
I have choked on this lifeless air
for many days, as California burns —
despair, a noose
tightening around my neck.

The bus rumbles down the road,
and then, I spot them —
a few wandering down the rows
of a farmer's cornfield.
With long, graceful necks and legs,
their grey bodies and wings relaxed,
they amble and eat
among autumn stalks
now cut to stubs —
saunter through patches of muddy water
with mates and young ones.
As the bus slows to a stop,
two cranes suddenly
face each other,
flap their wings in a joyful dance
millions of years old.
Delighted, my heart jumps too,
until I realize I am a prisoner —
peering at them through window glass,
protected from the acrid air they breathe,
unable to hear the soft trill of their voices.

I covet their dangerous freedom—
long to dance their dance,
learn their low, guttural cry.
I need to hear them call each other home,
call *me* home,
but it is getting late,
and the angry sun has almost set.
As the bus rumbles down the road,
I taste brackish water
in my parched mouth—
then realize it is tears.

After Hearing That the Camp Fire
is Almost Contained…

The Japanese maple is on fire.
I tell myself I am a poet who can change
the images in my head, but I can't
stop seeing the branches explode.
Each leaf is a burning tongue
lapping up sky —
the tree a huge fireball
racing through my backyard
towards our house.

Heart in my throat,
I look down the driveway.
The tall sweetgum trees have ignited too,
burning out of control
along the neighbor's fence line.
Out the living room window,
another maple smolders gold.
I am surrounded by flames
and for a horrible moment I panic —

Imagine I am going to die.
I escape to the back porch
and smell last night's rain,
feel the fine mist in my hair.
I stomp out a flame
burning on the ground —
then realize it is only a soggy autumn leaf,
stuck to the bottom of my shoe.

I go back into the kitchen and make coffee —
recite elegies for the dead.
Out the window,
what looks like wisps of smoke
just beyond a neighbor's rooftop,
is really the morning fog
rising up from the strait —
touching the wet hills
with its long, grey fingers.

Mountain Lion

Rounding a curve
out of Angel's Camp
in the summer twilight,
our car windows rolled down.
Inhaling the scent of pine trees
still warm from the afternoon sun
with slivers of moon
stuck in their boughs —
it's then we saw him...
not a deer
caught in the headlights' glare,
bewildered and frozen in its sprint,
but a mountain lion.
A tawny and muscular god,
he bounded out in front of us
and across the two-lane road
with the grace and ease of a dancer
leaping across a darkened stage.
Solitary and arrogant,
only after he reached the top
of the embankment in a single jump
did he turn for half a second —
his backward glance so bold and direct

as human and wild animal eyes met,
and locked briefly.
In his stare
a language understood between us
but not spoken—
before he silently turned away
and stealthily stalked the night.

Two Hawks

in memory of Mary Oliver

I think you might've known
when I looked up
at that cloudy smudge of grey
if it was two hawks I saw—
how they glided effortlessly
above the freeway,
smoothly criss-crossed
each other on the wind's breath.
I don't think
they were hunting
for prey—
the freeway below too congested
with cars and trucks,
nor were they hungering
for the rare roadkill,
for what had already died.
Just a joyful dance
between the two of them,
the black silhouettes
of their wings
almost touching.
You would have understood

in the glimpse of an eye
who they were,
and followed them up
into the wet hills
gladdened by rain,
while I, confined in my steel cage,
drove home
towards an empty sky.

Ode to Basho

At 3 a.m. the full moon is so bright,
it turns my window blinds into lanterns,
glowing white from the outside in.
Suddenly, strange thumping sounds
on the upstairs deck
and like a frightened child,
I peer through the crack between the glass and the shade
to see what lurks in the shadows —
only to find two rotund
black masked raccoons
moon gazing at the top of the steps,
like two venerable Japanese poets
reciting Basho to each other
under stars and planets —
sharing an almost
empty bottle of sake,
foraged from the garbage can
in the alley.

Then, I think to myself:
This should be me
sitting on the same steps —
slightly tipsy and in good spirits,
repeating the lines of the ancient master,
watching the full moon rise and set.

Where are you, my old friend,
on such a beautiful night?

Inside Out Love

It takes courage
to turn yourself inside out —
to wear your grey, muted side facing out,
and not feel embarrassed or apologize.
No overblown pink roses
blooming on your chest.
No bold blue stripes
running down your arms.
Forget the dazzling, polychromatic self
you want them to admire.
Instead, give that brightness to
your shy, aloof soul,
the one inside who sometimes feels colorless.
Cover it with repeated images
of magenta and turquoise birds,
persimmon butterflies and autumn paisley.

It takes courage
to show them your inside self —
to let them discover your blurry side,
the *you* that has no discernible pattern,
your brand name faded beyond recognition —
your inner self made of cloth

that has been softened by tears.
But note your seams are straight and true,
Label yourself
DURABLE, LASTING.
Tell them
with your loud,
beating heart
exposed —
that even *this* world,
this frightened, desperate world
we live in —
can be turned
inside out
with love.

Your Hands

for Sam

Your hands,
larger than life,
speak unspoken languages.
Instead of writing words,
they draw diagrams around my heart,
knowing what parts are needed
to make me whole.

Your hands fix things
that seem too hard to fix.
Survivors of a lost art,
they sand floors into amber rivers
smooth as glass.
Even my heart shines again,
lying tumbled and polished
in your stained palms.

Your hands know how
to open the maker's window.
Throbbing colors spill out
onto yards of blank canvas,
and the green worm of life

winds around your paintbrush.
Your hands paint rainbow spirits
and red-winged blackbirds.
They remember what color love is.

The blues groan in your hands,
moan in your hands
like a satisfied lover.
As one hand caresses your harp,
I imagine you stroking me over and over,
my thighs singing in anticipation.

Your hands are huge,
flesh-colored starfish,
slipping over my breasts
during low tide.
Your hands cupped together
offer me fresh water,
more than enough to stay alive.

Birthday Poem

Happy birthday to you
who are abrupt, unapologetic —
a jolt of caffeine to the universe,
a perfectly arrogant top that spins
around me and never stops.

When you are with me,
our season is always summer.
Your eyes —
an unending blue, cloudless glance,
bring on the sweat of an August afternoon,
a longing for cool white cotton on the skin.

Happy birthday to you
who are stubborn, steadfast —
a hardy volunteer flower,
perhaps poppy or calla lily,
whose tender kisses
blossom year after year
around my mouth.

Happy birthday to you
who are strong, straightforward—
a builder of sheds and showers and kitchen counters,
the man who has hammered our imperfect lives together.
Perpendicular, that's a good word you say.
The beginning of a window, I think—
an opening for light.

Afternoon Nap

While you sleep in the reclining chair,
the warmth from the afternoon sun
softens the lines in your face.
Your head tilts to one side,
and your chest rises with relaxed breaths —
as if in a dream you have finally found
what you have been looking for
your whole life,
and with your hand
resting over your heart,
you protect it.

Roots

In the dry heat
of an August afternoon,
we carry pots of succulents
up to the top deck and clear
the long redwood planter box
of the spindly star jasmine
that has grown sparse and old.
The round succulent buds
will take its place and thrive,
in spite of drought and probable neglect.

It is a tedious job,
pulling out the old growth,
and you do it impatiently.
I wonder if you want
to get it over with because
you know how it feels
to be torn loose, displaced,
to float down into callous space.
Suddenly, I want to kiss you,
take you to bed and press tendrils
of your long hair into my pillow;
whisper my promise that
you will never be uprooted.

Instead, I let you pull up roots,
tangled and jumbled
as a head of hair,
while I toss the dirt
clumps over the railing
and watch them settle
like abandoned nests
on the bushes in the yard.

I think about my roots,
how they have curled and
moaned in every crack and
crevice of this house
for thirty years,
how my toes wiggle down
beyond the basement floor,
below the hard foundation,
into somewhere dark and knowing
where there is no loss.

After the Poetry Reading

This is one way I remember us —
listening to the clatter of plates and bowls
at a Chinese restaurant.
Your gaze catches
the gold koi
swimming on the wall behind me,
then lets them loose —
unlike me, who circles frantically in your net.

Across the street, *Flowerland* is closed.
I'd like to run away to a place with that name —
find a lover with the delicate
purple mouth of an orchid
who would let me grow wild.
Instead, I eat lemon chicken soaked in honey,
and pork chow mein —
the noodles shiny with oil,
the onions translucent.
You finish your tea;
I take a last sip of wine.

I tell myself we have never understood
how to communicate with each other.
These words I don't know how to say
as silent as your icy blue eyes
staring beyond the window.

Perhaps you imagine the bouquet
of deep, red roses
you will surprise me with tomorrow —
each flower as speechless
as my mouth,
opening for a kiss.

Forecast

Afternoon
thickens and darkens
on winter's vine.

Sallow leaves weep
on rose bushes.

Naked tree branches
splinter cold light
into jagged pieces
of dulled glass.

Cracks of blue sky
are sutured —
leaving a pale skin
of grey clouds.

The forecast says rain.
I hibernate under blankets—
dream that misaligned planets
will right themselves,
that the world will continue.

The day smells of wet roses.
It runs ahead of me —
disappears before I can catch it.

The gift we are given
is never quite knowing
when something beautiful
will begin or end.

The rosebud you gave me
kept in a small, wooden box —
its petals
brittle, yellow, perfect.

I Bring You Roses

for Sam

I bring you roses —
creamy white, lemon yellow,
deep red, and mauve.
Carefully, I cut the stems and put them
in a glass vase filled with clear water —
let you see the stems drink
and the leaves flush green,
the petals soften and swell.

You ask me to explain
why the flowers never fully open,
as if each perfectly shaped bud
is carved in wax.
Why the petals on the red one
release a small breath,
and as their edges curl under
never breathe again.
Why the yellow rose lets one soft petal drop
as the rest stiffen
and crumble to the touch.
Why the white one droops its head
and dies prematurely,
leaving no scent.

Silently, I take you to the garden
where the sun nudges the roses awake,
and each flower welcomes bugs and bees.
As the buds explode open,
I show you how the petals
ripen and fall to the ground,
their warm, sweet scent in our nostrils —
how our kisses blossom in the garden
where the roses grow wild.

Lovers in the Red Sky

a painting by Marc Chagall

The sky is a red
of the deepest passion —
the scarlet blush on a woman's lips
after being kissed.
Two lovers form a comet's head,
her long white skirt a blazing tail
trailing across a humid sky,
the town below asleep,
unaware of this bliss,
this selfless innocence
captured in a painting
a child might have drawn.
The wedding portrait
of a man and woman
floating in a circular embrace
their arms wrapped around each other
as two arms hold one spirit.
The sacred circle of a wedding ring,
the whimsy of a loyal horse,
whose human hands

offer a bouquet of fidelity.
The man and woman fly unashamed—
her round breasts smile like moons
shining on a bird singing into their mouths.

After Seeing a Painting by Monet

I wander into his painting—
smell the warm scent of
an August afternoon,
the air heavy with desire.
The old painter, almost blind,
paints a season I have forgotten.
I sit among the purple agapanthus
and orange blood lilies that bloom on his canvas—
water grasses reflected in his failing eyes
brush against my arms.
I take off my clothes
and float naked in his pond,
my nipples blossoming
among his pink waterlilies.
My body, a moist flower,
opening passionately
under his violet sky—
then becoming the white mist,
rising, rising,
to meet it.

A Geisha's Lament

I am the discreet one,
who quietly enters the steaming onsen
and lets the thin blue and white yakata
fall from her shoulders.

I am the lovely one,
whose body is a perfectly curved shell,
curling silently into itself.

I am the patient one,
who gazes out at the garden,
looking for a shadow moving
across the dark pines.

I am the sad one,
who sees only a deer
grazing in the moonlit meadow grasses.

I am the lonely one,
whose lover is a cruel dream.

In the empty pool
my hands are small fish,
shimmering motionless in the moonlight.

The Muse

She always knew
it would be a bird
that appeared—
a seagull, grey and white as waves,
a muse who smelled of fish and salt,
or the green moss that
grows on wet rocks.
Such a tender dream,
the gull who flew down
and protected her,
who became the crown that adorned her head—
its wings, laurel branches of wisdom,
a strong beak pointed toward her heart.
At last she understood.
She cupped her hands and made a nest
to hold all the hungry little fledglings
so eager to fly—
the new words crying out.

Dream Poem for Li-Young Lee

In her dream
she repeats his name
like a sacred mantra,
bites into his name
the way she would eat
a juicy nectarine,
lets his poems run down
the back of her throat
and become her poems.

Suddenly, he takes her by the arm
and steers her through
the crowded streets
of Chinatown —
the hot midnight air
steamy with the scent of pork buns
and thick with firework smoke,
a red dragon twisting
on the street corner.
It's a new year and in the sky,
a star dog laps up tears
from the moon's shallow bowl.

The poet whispers
the language of flowers
into her ear.
She hears the sound
of purple irises weeping.
White chrysanthemum petals
fall into her hair like snow.
She is wearing a long skirt
the color of young bamboo shoots.
He is wearing black,
his hair pulled into a knot of sorrow.

They walk down dark alleys
which become winding rivers of memory.
They talk about the paper-thin delicacy
of wasp wings.

They eat his favorite fruit,
ripe peaches,
and the night blossoms in their fingers.

They stand under a sky
the color of bruised plums.
Face turned upward,
she opens her mouth
to swallow fluttering rose petals
which become tears
which become words for a poem.

As he walks away from her,
he holds a peach in his hand
and it glows —
a small sun
caught in a lantern of stars.

Postcards from a Dream

She rises up in a whirlwind
from her own dream —
a goddess in a gown
of indigo nights and embroidered moons.

The face of an old shaman
floats by —
he knows her name
and silently loves her.

Swirling, twirling, whirling,
she dances high above the village.
In her hand she holds a quill
she calls *the eye of God* —
writes postcards from a dream,
then lets them flutter down —
fallen stars upon the ground.

Books

Someday people will ask
what it felt like to hold a book,
to run a finger down its spine,
to inhale the woody odor of paper,
to touch the words reverently,
as if they were blessings.

The last of the Old Ones
will remember them fondly
and speak in whispers
of what has been banned,
burned, or buried alive.
They will call books
the ancient artifacts of truth.
They will refer to them fondly
as *those tiny birds' feet,*
those thin gasps of knowledge
we once tracked across a barren desert,
the tracks now lost, covered in sand.

They will still keep a few
in their hidden bookshelves —
the spines toppled over,
the pages scattered.
The ruins of abandoned cities
and the scribble of a dying language
gathering dust —
the sound of wings written down
after the last bird has disappeared.

Palm Reader

You carry your life's journey
in the palm of your hand,
the same way I see it
in the lines of your face
or in your blue veins —
rivers of blood, coursing to the heart.
It's all here, she tells me,
gently caressing the lines in my palm —
from the first breath
to the last incredulous moan.

I stare at the curving lines,
knowing I haven't wasted my life,
just meandered along many paths —
a traveler who has never
followed signposts.

Scattered moments I have tried
to paint in my head —
a single sunset on the isle of Crete —
brilliant blue and orange,
a monoprint etched in my brain.

Caressing my first lover
under a sleeping bag
in the vestry of an old church—
a glissando of spring rain
tapping on the roof.

Idle talk over coffee
at a kitchen table in a small apartment—
two mismatched mugs leaving rings
of conversation and spilled cream
on a blue and white checked tablecloth—
smoke of clove cigarettes
sweetening the air.

I feel the ache of autumn in my fingers,
and stare again at the lines of my journey,
never asking her how many years are left.
Each line a river, and I,
a silver fish swimming
towards the sea.

A Room of One's Own

for Virginia Woolf

1.

You did not choose madness to be your muse.
All you wanted was a room facing seaward
with stark white windows flung wide open,
a quiet place to write the words
that floated into your brain
like tangled sea grass, the smell of salt
carried on late afternoon ocean breezes,
filling your nostrils with a giddy freedom.

2.

Did you lock the door behind you
when you penned those extraordinary novels
simmering in your awkward heart?
Were you really the defiant unconventional canary,
trilling stubbornly day after day
inside some claustrophobic space,
perched high and solitary
in the confines of a second story
room, gazing out a small rectangular

window at perhaps the corner
of a dingy brick building
or a piece of windless sky?

Did the midnight streetlights
puncture your tender wings
as you escaped through the small crack
of an open window, your image mirrored
in a pane of streaked glass?
You, a wounded bird, now at last liberated,
spread your blood-tinged wings towards the Atlantic,
unwritten words, tiny soft feathers
drifting down like crimson snow.

3.

Virginia, that day in March
when your frayed dreams finally unraveled,
when you chose to fill your pockets
with heavy stones and walk
into the cold dark river,
did you for a brief second
dare to imagine yourself reborn?
That even though the manuscript lay unfinished,
the room no longer yours,
the songbird's heart crushed,
you would vow to return someday to sit with me
and with other women who dream of water,
who choose their words carefully,
who write in other rooms.

Water Lilies

Her first memory was of water lilies.
At two years old, she took
her mother's hand
and led her passionately
to the long reflecting pool
behind the old French hotel.
It was a daily fascination, obsession,
to view the perfect white flowers —
fallen stars from last night's sky
that floated among dark green moon leaves
on the surface of still water.
Cup-shaped and tinged a delicate pink,
they opened for her every morning —
embraced sunlight the same way
her own small hands opened up
to grasp the first pieces of the day.

She would solemnly return
at dusk to watch their petals close up,
as if they were protecting something
lovely inside themselves
that was still untouched —
the pool turning into black marble,

impenetrable but infinite,
reflecting a billion silver lilies
blooming light years away—
her pale hands reaching up,
becoming five pointed stars.

Isabelle

After all these years,
I finally cradle your photograph
in hand and wonder who
you really were.
All the women
and men who loved you
are gone —
your story gone with them.

Your looks do not resemble mine.
You, great grandmother,
born of German father and French mother,
have pale white skin,
curly hair pulled up into a soft cloud.
I admire your strong jaw,
how your dark handsome eyes
stare out beyond mine
at something I will never see.

Nor will you again
place the summer's pink peonies
in a porcelain vase,
or have your husband
touch the ruffled black lace
falling off your shoulder.

Your beauty,
long preserved in platinum light
remains unchanged,
framed and circled
with tiny round pearls
and tarnished silver flowers—
while Indiana starlight
stays the same
and keeps your secrets for eternity.

Isabelle,
except for the faintest
hint of smile,
you leave me nothing.
I wish I had your name.

The Gift

in memory of my mother

In those first days
I kept my poems hidden,
let them ripen in notebooks
like a strange fruit that was not
quite ready to be eaten.
One year for your birthday
I gathered eight of them together,
sing-song typed them on thin rice paper,
hole punched and placed them
in a paper folder the color of sunflowers.
Each poem bloomed in silence,
waiting to be read.
Years passed—
you never mentioned the poems
and neither did I,
assuming I had disappointed you.
After you died,
I found the folder and took it back,
stuck it between books on a shelf
like a love letter I had never mailed.
You had written my name on the front cover,
my childhood name, printed in black ink

and underlined.
Tonight, I open the folder and read
each poem out loud,
wondering if somewhere on a page
your invisible fingerprints linger,
listening.

It Wasn't Your Fault

Years later,
I am here to tell you
in the way only a mother can,
that it wasn't your fault
your dog got hit by a car
and died that April morning
when you were eight.
The world was still full of promise —
when until that moment,
you had never known death.

It wasn't your best friend's fault either,
though you blamed her —
the gate left open,
both of you excited
to go to Disneyland for the first time,
running in and out of the yard —
and your pure happiness
precluded caution.

How were you to know
we spin the wheel of chance
throughout our lives—
that we are blind to the signs of tragedy,
and like you and your dog,
ignore danger and follow joy.

Forgive yourself and your friend—
forgive your dog too.
It is in our natures,
both animal and human
to make that choice—
to run out that open gate
and keep going.

How the Dream Comes

for Cassie

It doesn't matter how the dream comes,
just that it comes, and it always does.
Poverty, heartbreak, or abuse might defer it,
but it still finds a way to slip inside you
and begin its song.
Sometimes it first appears when you're a little girl,
maybe five or six years old.
You see a tiny bold bird,
flitting from branch to branch
among leaves of gold
and know it is you,
ready to fly to the highest point
in the sky and disappear.

Perhaps the dream finds you at school—
floats just outside the classroom window,
just beyond the teacher's glance—
a ripple of rainbow light,
an impatient kite,
yes, that's you too!

Sometimes, the dream doesn't settle
in your heart until you're older,
maybe in your thirties.
It's the whisper, the yearning
you can't quite put your finger on,
but it's there.
It calls to you late at night
after you've put the children to bed,
or arrived home exhausted from work.
It knows you better than any lover,
and you may find that over time,
you will spend many hours alone
without family or friends
just to embrace it.

What matters is that you
follow this dream.
Breathe it in as if it's your last breath,
your only hope.
Love what is turbulent and wild in you —
a shell tumbling inside
the ocean's waves.
And when you finally become your dream,
fill your lungs with it —
belt it out to the world!
Let all those who have yet to dream
hear your raucous song,

and look for that tiny, bold bird
winging fearlessly
towards an open sky.

How to Celebrate my Life

El Dia de los Muertos

The first year after I die,
celebrate my life
on my birthday—
El Dia de los Muertos.
Set up an altar
in the living room,
under the Rivera painting
of the woman embracing
the white calla lilies.
Put everything on that
heavy carved wooden
table next to the window.
Light a church candle
with an ornate picture of
the Madonna of Guadalupe
wrapped around the glass
to help me find my way home.
Tempt me with a round loaf
of sweet Mexican bread
covered with candy sprinkles,
pan de muerto.
I want a ghoulish turquoise

skull with bright orange marigold eyes
to sit on the table and grin at you
as you walk by, my former smile
hidden behind its clacking teeth.
Leave me a plate of soft, gooey brie,
and a box of Carr's water crackers.
Cleanse my palate with a silky red cabernet,
and don't forget the cut crystal goblet.
Fill a clear vase of yellow roses
with your tears. A simple ceramic
bowl of salt and seashells will
remind me of the ocean.
Place my favorite *calaca*, the skeleton
dog wearing the violet *sombrero*,
next to an open book of Haiku.
Read her a poem about longing and a full moon.
Call her *perro de mi corazon*.
If my friends are still alive, invite them over.
Hire a loud, mariachi band and
dance all night to Rolling Stones cover songs.

Place all my poems on the altar.
Let each friend take a few
until the stack is gone.
Tell them the blank sides are good
for writing lists.
The living like to do that.
At midnight, take off your shoes,
peel off your skin, and
rest your tired bones.
Stay a while. Remind me,
that I'm really not alone.

Transmigration

As I stood at the end of the pier
and looked out,
sunlight glittered a path to
the other shore.
I imagined a flock of birds —
brilliant diamonds of light
skimming across ripples
of blue water,
the same color as sky.

Water became endless sky.

I imagined a thousand shining leaves
drifting down a river —
sterling silver leaves
the same color
as the moon's glassy-eyed tears.

Leaves became tears.

I imagined a kaleidoscope
of silver butterflies,
sparkling and flitting across the strait,
wings as delicate as a last breath.

Butterflies became flutters of breath.

A glistening goodbye
from souls who slipped away
into light,
into sighs,
those birds,
those leaves,
those butterflies.

Your Voice the Sound of Waves

in memory of Frances Jackson

In the softness of early morning,
I sit by the water and remember you.

The strait is as smooth as green bottle glass,
the breezy edges of what will be a hot day, still cool.

You wrote poems for the ocean —
the power and beauty of the tides,
the miracle of our salty beginnings.

Your eyes saw explosions of turquoise and sapphire
as waves and whitecaps churned and crashed,
salt spray brushed onto a canvas of summer sky.

Somewhere in that wildness was music,
a passionate tango you danced —
coral pink sea flowers pinned in your hair.

You listened to those ancient mariner ghosts,
how they moaned in the hulls of the sunken sailing ships,
how they begged you to read them your lines.

If I had your poems,
I would copy them carefully on small pieces of driftwood
salvaged from last year's winter storms —
then toss them into the waves off Mendocino or Monterey.

I'd watch your words float away
to become tangled in seaweed,
or braided with shells into a mermaid's necklace.

This morning and forever after,
your voice the sound of waves
caressing mossy rocks.

In Memory of a Poet

for L.C.

You died while I wasn't paying attention.
You died while I was absent-mindedly
making dinner, burning the pork chops black,
or maybe while I was sending an invitation
to twenty poets, your name included on the list.
I didn't hear your last breath,
unless it was disguised as the strong wind
that whistled through the cracks
of my house at dusk.

While you slipped away,
I straightened up the bed,
watched the five o'clock news,
flossed my teeth,
oblivious that your heart was
pumping out its last beats.
No hierophant interpreted
the coffee grounds floating in my cup,
no dream whispered to me
that you had lost your North Star.

Tonight, I can't write,
so I fold laundry and think of you.
The dead disappear like missing socks—
we keep hoping they'll turn up again
and look for them in the strangest places,
especially in the folded-up pieces of ourselves.

I tell myself that from now on
I will pay more attention,
meet old friends for coffee,
memorize phone numbers,
read love poems out loud.
It's been three days,
and my train of thought has been derailed.
There's mud on the tracks
and my trip has been cancelled.
What will I do in the meantime?
That's the question the living always ask the dead—
What will I do now?

Prayer

To whom it may concern:
I have sent you a message,
an invocation written
on the tails of shooting stars
to wrap your flame
around this dark hull of earth
and ignite the dormant seed within.
Let the heat of love
burn away all winter's horrors —
turn dead leaves into flowers,
and darkness into light.

As This Day Fades

As this day fades away
without regret of leaving,
notice how passionately
the trees blow kisses
to the white-shelled turtle
who paddles across
the smooth blue pond of sky.

Remember the persistent ache of joy,
how love needles old bones awake
and waxes inside the lung
like a breathing moon,
grown too large and luminous
to ignore.

Kneel down,
touch your head to the earth —
become the old soul
humbled once again
by the leap
of a billion stars.

A Tiny Bird Called Hope

in memory of Joel Fallon

Hope is the thing with feathers
that perches in the soul
Emily Dickinson

If such a tiny bird,
perhaps left for dead
or suffering from an injured wing,
its feathers matted and torn,
finds refuge in your broken heart,
then reach inside yourself
and touch this living thing called Hope.
Gently bind its limp and useless wing
with Love's tattered cloth,
and press it to your shattered heart
until it heals,
until this lovely creature sings again.
Then let it fly,
and nest in someone else's heart,
the stranger,
the neighbor,
the old friend,
the one who just like you,
needs to hear its song.